MARRIED The Same Man TWICE

LaTanya Williams.

Dedication

This book is first dedicated to **God**, my Refuge, my Strength, and my Healer.

When my heart was broken, you held me together.

When I didn't understand the pain, you gave it purpose.

Everything I survived, every lesson I learned, and every word written here is because of Your grace.

This book is also dedicated to my sons, **Lamar and Lamont Jr.**

You are my reason for choosing healing over bitterness and strength over surrender.

I hope my story shows you the power of faith, boundaries, and self-worth.

Everything I do is to leave you an example of resilience, courage, and unwavering trust in God.

Introduction

Hello, my name is Latanya and I've experienced not one but two divorces. This book was written from the broken pieces that God healed. I never imagined my life would unfold the way it did. I did not enter both relationships expecting betrayal, heartache, or pain. I entered with commitment and love thinking things would work even when the warning signs were loud. I loved deeply and stayed longer than I should have.

I trusted people that did not protect my heart. My love story includes loss, betrayal, divorce and deep emotional wounds, but it also includes survival, growth, boundaries, and restoration. This book is about what happens when God meets you in the middle of your mess and walks you out with wisdom, strength, and clarity. I shar my story not to shame anyone, but to free someone. I learned lessons the hard way, through ignored red flags, emotional entanglements, broken trust, and seasons where I questioned my worth. Every tear eventually became my testimony. In my healing season after divorce, God began writing my story. He taught me that love is not consuming, boundaries are biblical, and peace is necessary. Walking away can sometimes be obedient not failure. If you are reading this while healing from betrayal, divorce, heartbreak, or emotional exhaustion this book is for you. May these pages remind you that healing is possible, peace is promised, and your story is still being written.

Table of Contents

When my Boyfriend became my husband and the warning signs I Ignored.

I was young when my boyfriend became my husband—too young to understand what marriage truly required or how seriously God viewed the covenant. I was only twenty years old, full of hope, belief, and love, but lacking wisdom and discernment. I ignored the warning signs because I wanted the relationship to work more than I wanted to face the truth. I believed love could fix what character would not change.

I met him through my best friend; he was her cousin. At that age, that connection felt safe and familiar. I trusted him partly because of who introduced us, not because of what he consistently showed me. What I didn't understand then was that proximity and familiarity do not equal integrity.

Before we ever got married, the cheating had already started. Some of it came through rumors, some I discovered on my own, and some truth came out years later. One of the deepest betrayals happened before we were married, when I found out he had slept with a close friend—someone who knew my heart, my struggles, and my loyalty. When I found out, me and that friend got into a fight. Years later, I learned the truth through her cousins. It hurt deeply knowing that so many people knew before I did.

I stayed with him, but I stopped talking to her. Later, after I was no longer with him, I chose to forgive her. Forgiveness didn't mean what happened was acceptable—it meant I refused to carry bitterness into my future.

Despite all of this, I still married him while he was incarcerated. Looking back, that alone was a warning sign, but at the time I believed loyalty meant standing by him no matter what. He had already cheated on me repeatedly and had children by other women before we ever said our vows. The truth was right in front of me, but I chose hope over evidence. I believed marriage would change him.

Near the end of our relationship, he went to jail again—the last time. Because we were married, I thought we should finally have our own place. I believed starting fresh might bring stability, so before he came home, I got us our first apartment. I was trying to build something real. But when he came home, he returned to the same fast life and street mentality. Nothing changed. That was the moment I got tired—tired of waiting, tired of hoping, and tired of being hurt.

I stayed with him for eight years. When I finally decided to leave, he began stalking me and the man I was dating at the time. One day, he pulled us over while he had a gun in the car. Years later, he admitted to me that his plan that day was to kill us both. What I thought was heartbreak was actually God's protection.

He lived a fast street life—drugs, poor decisions, and constantly being in and out of jail. I eventually met someone else and began dating that man. One day, when I was ready for my husband to move out, I tried to cut his clothes with a knife. In my anger, I cut my own hand badly. God does not like ugly, and I received the consequences quickly. I ended up needing surgery to repair a tendon in my hand.

That physical pain healed, but the emotional pain followed me into the next season of my life. Much later, during another painful divorce, God required me to finally sit still and reflect. I had to look honestly at the two relationships I had been in and ask myself where I went wrong.

Why did I allow these men to repeatedly cheat on me? Was I insecure within myself? Why did I forgive so easily without taking time to heal? Through that reflection, I realized the truth—I married the same man twice, just in different bodies. I did not heal from the first relationship, and because of that, I repeated the same cycle.

This time, I am choosing differently. I am choosing healing before love. I am taking the time to grow, to learn, and to break the pattern so I do not repeat the cycle a third time.

The warning signs were always there. I just wasn't ready to honor them yet. Now I am.

And that has made all the difference.

This chapter represents one of the most painful yet eye-opening seasons of my life. Staying with someone for eight years who repeatedly showed me who he was forced me to confront hard truths—not just about him, but about myself. Loving someone should never put your life at risk, and realizing how close I came to danger changed everything for me.

When I finally chose to walk away, I learned that leaving does not always bring instant peace. His stalking, the gun, and the later confession about his plan revealed how serious the situation truly was. What I once thought was heartbreak was actually God's protection. I can now say with confidence that God didn't just save my heart—He saved my life.

Healing required me to sit still and reflect on the patterns I ignored and the boundaries I never set. I had to ask myself why I stayed so long, why I forgave so easily, and why I believed love meant endurance instead of safety and peace. These were not easy questions, but they were necessary ones.

Through reflection, I learned that unresolved pain has a way of repeating itself. Because I did not take the time to heal from my first marriage, I found myself marrying the same man again—only in a different body. That realization became a turning point in my life.

This season of healing is different. I am no longer rushing ahead of God. I am no longer ignoring warning signs. I am choosing to pause, to heal, and to grow so that I do not repeat the cycle again. Reflection taught me that breaking generational and relational patterns requires honesty, patience, and surrender.

If you see yourself in this chapter, know this: leaving does not make you weak—it makes you wise. Healing is not punishment; it is preparation. And sometimes God allows us to see the danger behind us so we never walk back into it again.

This chapter is not just about what I survived. It is about how I learned, healed, and chose better. And that choice has changed my life.

5

The Weight of Repeated Betrayal

Going into a new relationship with a different man but dealing with the same problems was the result of jumping from one relationship to the next without taking time to heal from the first trauma. I did not take the time to heal and learn, so I went through the exact same struggles with the same type of man—just in a different body.

That second person came in and temporarily took the pain away, but my judgment was clouded. A new person can numb the pain, but they cannot heal the wounds left behind from a previous relationship. Because I never addressed what needed to be healed, the cycle continued.

That second relationship started off wrong from the very beginning because we were both married to other people. God did not have His hand on that relationship because of the foundation it was built on. The woman I am today would never date a married man. I know better now. That is adultery. Back then, I was too young to fully understand what adultery truly meant. I had been in church my whole life, but at twenty-three years old, I didn't really know any better.

Like the Bible says, *"Forgive them, for they know not what they do."* I knew there was a God, and I went to church because I was raised in church, but I probably couldn't quote scripture back then except for the Lord's Prayer. I was still clubbing and going to church at the same time, but the messages would go in one ear and out the other.

I still attend the same church today. I've been going there since 1999. He was not someone who was into church like I was. I don't even know if he knew I was married at the time, but he did know I was in a relationship. What I didn't find out until months later was that *he* was married. By the time I found out, we were already deeply involved.

I never took the time to ask the hard questions. I assumed that if a man was pursuing me and spending a lot of time with me, he didn't have a girlfriend or a wife. I know better now. Today, you have to ask direct questions—are you engaged, married, emotionally involved, bisexual, or anything else that matters before getting emotionally attached. Even then, some people will still lie because they want what they want, all while having a whole wife and kids at home.

That's why discernment is so important. Pay close attention to red flags, especially in the beginning. Stop giving people passes when you catch them in lies, particularly during the dating stage. What you ignore early on will always resurface later.

After these two men, I knew I needed a break to heal so I wouldn't keep repeating the same cycles. Sometimes we have to look at ourselves and ask why we allowed certain things to continue. Yes, people hurt us, but we choose to stay and keep expecting them to change. Some never do.

Right now, I am focusing on God while I grow and heal so I will not repeat this cycle a third time. If I don't heal, I already know how that story would end—probably with a second book, part two.

Back then, I didn't hear terms like *red flags*. The red flags from these two men practically slapped me in the face, yet I stayed. I thank God that I am not damaged by what I went through. They took me through it, just like the song says—but now, I can laugh about it.

As I stated before, we had problems from the very beginning, dealing with his ex and mine stalking us and causing issues. I know they were both hurting because their significant others left them. I couldn't imagine a man just getting up and leaving me. Thank God I have never experienced that. I was the one who eventually left both of them once I got tired of the toxicity.

I know his wife at the time took it hard.

She was pregnant and already had a younger child. The woman I am today would never date a married man. I don't care if they've been separated for a while—why haven't you gotten a divorce? I don't care if the court date is the next day; call me when it's finalized. I don't play with God like that. I was immature back then, but now I know better. I'm not about to mess up my blessing.

Women and men need to learn how serious God is about marriage. I once heard a woman on social media say—on a talk show—that she was attracted to married men. The fact that she stood in front of a crowd and said that was mind-blowing to me.

At one point, I started to think that God was punishing me because of me and him being married. But I later learned it had nothing to do with me—it was all on him. That was the kind of person he was. I would ask myself why this man was treating me the way he did, like there was something wrong with me or like it was our fault. But I later heard he did his first wife so badly too. That's when I realized it had nothing to do with me at all. It was a reflection of his character.

I recently learned that you recognize a person by their fruit (Matthew 7:15–20). He was a bad tree that bore bad fruit. It wasn't just one man—it was both men's character issues. It had nothing to do with my worth. They could have been good men if they made better choices, but they didn't. Street men tend to live fast lives and juggle multiple women. When you hang with fools, you become a fool. When all your homeboys are cheating on their women, you become a follower and do what they do.

After we divorced, I spoke with one of his aunts, and she didn't even know we were divorced. She said when she heard we were getting married, she thought to herself, *why is this girl marrying him?* Now when someone's own aunt says that, that speaks volumes. She went on to say he had done his first wife so badly. If nobody really knows you, your family definitely does. She had been around him his whole life, so she knew exactly who he was.

I remember the very first time I experienced his temper. My ex was standing on my side of the car trying to talk to me. I barely rolled my window down because at that point I was done with him. This new boyfriend pulled up and completely lost control. They fought right there. Guns were pulled—thank God no one was hurt. I got out of the car, and that man grabbed me by my neck. A friend had to pull him off of me.

That was the very beginning. That was the first red flag showing he had no self-control. I even tried to explain to him that I wasn't talking to my ex and that my window was barely down, but he wasn't trying to hear that.

Seventeen years later, after all the toxic mess this man took me through, I still ended up marrying him in 2018. Same situation as the first man—they do not change when you get married. Looking back, it's crazy. He waited seventeen years to marry me. And let me be clear: I am marriage material. I always have been, and I always will be. He was just too immature—then and now.

He was still married to his first wife up until 2017, the year before we got married. When I left my first husband, I divorced him immediately. I wasn't about to stay legally married to someone I was no longer with—that's ridiculous. I asked him over and over again in the beginning to get a divorce, but eventually I got tired of asking and stopped bringing it up. We were together, so I pushed it to the back of my mind.

Men like that usually don't go to court unless they're forced to—unless it's mandatory for a case they have. Later in the relationship, after one of our breakups, I finally put my foot down.

So, let's go back to the beginning.

It was a long time. I was with this man for twenty-three years before I finally walked away—that's half of my life. This man caused me the most pain I have ever experienced. Almost the entire twenty-three years were bad, except for maybe the first two years. We had fun and good times in the beginning, but the bad eventually outweighed the good.

I dealt with the same problems I had experienced in my first relationship: in and out of jail, street life, drugs, cheating, and being with an emotionally unstable man. The only thing he didn't do was have children on me, at least not that I knew of. I stayed through all the other cheating, but once we got married and he cheated, I was done.

Before we got married, when I gave him another chance, I told him we were starting fresh and leaving all the past mess behind us. I told him we could work through anything to save our marriage, but cheating was something I would not accept. By that time, he should have had all that cheating out of his system, but clearly, he didn't.

One reason God allows divorce is adultery, and that was my way out. I walked away, as painful as it was. I did not want a divorce, but I was not about to stay and allow someone to continue doing me wrong and cheating on me.

We met in 2001, back when I was clubbing in my early twenties. I had no kids at the time and was living my best life. Clubbing was part of that lifestyle. We were at clubs almost every day of the week, and I would still wake up and go to work. My body isn't like that anymore—if I go out during the week now, I'm not getting up for work. But I don't do clubs anymore anyway. My house is my club now. It's the only place I like to be, in peace.

I remember him whispering in my ear, *"I want you."* We exchanged numbers that night and started talking. We began hanging out and spending time together. Once I started liking him, I noticed I began acting differently toward my husband at the time. Eventually, I tried to put him out, and that was the day I cut my hand acting out in anger. Things went downhill from there. The whole relationship became a problem.

His wife started coming to my house looking for him and following us around. It was a lot to deal with. At times, I would tell him this was too much for me. I had never experienced baby mama drama or that level of chaos before. Me and him got along well in the beginning, outside of the issues with the exes. That new love phase made everything else feel distant.

We went everywhere together and were inseparable—matching outfits and all. We were good for about the first two years of the relationship. There were no cheating issues that I knew of or heard about, but he did go to jail within those first two years for about a year, or close to it.

Here I was again, with a new man, running back and forth to jails and putting my life on hold for someone making poor choices. I knew the lifestyle he lived, so I knew that came with the territory. I stayed loyal and faithful and rode it out with him.

In the beginning, he was quiet—or at least that's what I thought. That wasn't really him. He was presenting a version of himself he wanted me to believe was real. That mask fell off after he came home from jail the first time. I hadn't seen his emotional instability and anger issues yet, except for that one early incident. I let it go because I didn't realize then that he couldn't control his anger.

When he came home, he went straight back to the streets and caught another case within a year—one he stayed on the run from for three years. The day he got that case, we got into a big argument, and the police had to be called because of his temper.

And from there, it only got worse.

He was not physically abusive to me, but he had serious anger and temper issues. Because of one of his outbursts, his mother and sister ended up coming to our house. The argument started because I answered his phone, and when I said hello, the person hung up. Clearly, it had to be a female, and that sparked everything.

By this time, we were in our third year of dating, around 2004. I was in love and never thought about leaving over an argument. I was young and naïve and didn't look at the bigger picture of this man's temper. This was the second major anger incident after the first one, but there had been a gap of several years between them. To me, it was just an argument, and within a day or two, we moved on. What I failed to pay attention to was how extreme his reactions were and how emotionally unstable he truly was.

The longer you stay with a person, the harder it becomes to leave. That is something I understand now. That is why I am growing and healing, so I do not repeat the same cycle. I am learning to guard my heart and to recognize a person by their fruit. At that point, I had already invested years into the relationship, which made walking away even harder. When someone apologizes, we want to believe them—until apologies turn into patterns.

There is nothing anyone can do to hurt me going forward after the pain I experienced through this divorce. I know what pain feels like now, and I know I can survive it with God on my side. If God brought me out, He can bring you out too. I am walking away at the first sign of behavior I no longer accept. I am a better woman now, and I will never go through what I went through with those two men again.

By the time the police arrived that day, he had already taken off in his mother's truck. When the officers finally came for our call, they explained there had been another police situation on the main street in front of our apartments. A man had jumped out of a truck and ran, and officers saw him throw something. What they found turned out to be drugs.

Once we returned to talking about our situation, the officer started putting things together. It became clear my boyfriend was the man they were looking for. After the officer left, we went to the main street, and sure enough, it was his mother's truck, with police surrounding the area looking for him. He wasn't caught on that case until three years later, in 2007.

We moved immediately because they knew it was him. After that, his attitude became nasty, and he did the most because he thought my mother had told on him. As if they weren't going to figure it out anyway—it was his mom's truck. Of course, they were going to question her when she came to retrieve it, and they already had his name from our police call.

After that incident, he was hardly ever home. I felt like I couldn't say anything about the times he came in or his constant presence in the streets because I knew the lifestyle he lived when we got together. So, I stayed quiet and went with the flow. Did I like it? No. But I told myself, *this is what he does.*

The cheating started to become outrageous—constant phone calls and hang-ups. One day, we got into an argument, and I don't even remember what it was about, but he pulled a gun on me. Maybe I told him I was going to leave; I honestly don't remember. What's scary is how I didn't take that moment seriously enough to walk away. I brushed it off like it was nothing.

That wasn't the first time a gun was involved, but it was the first time he did it to me before we were married. The second time happened after we were married. We tend to overlook things like that because we convince ourselves that these men wouldn't really do anything.

But the truth is—they will, if the situation escalates.

Who gets that angry and pulls a gun on the person they claim to love? An unstable person. A close friend of mine lost her friend to this exact situation. Her husband was unstable, and she brushed his behavior off lightly. The week of her death, I told my friend that she needed to take the situation more seriously. I had met her a few times, and she was really sweet. From what I heard, she went through a lot with that husband, including physical abuse.

Ladies, it is unacceptable for a man or a woman to put their hands on you. That is not love. Get help and leave. A few days later, that man killed her. Rest in peace, Granny. Some people are truly unstable and will go to any extreme. Just recently, a man in Houston killed his pregnant girlfriend. These stories are real, and they happen more often than we want to believe.

I no longer take anything lightly when it comes to relationships. Discernment can save us from a lot of pain—and even save our lives. The sad part is that despite all those warning signs, I still stayed with him. I believe I was even pregnant at the time when we lived in that apartment.

After we had our first son, we moved again. We would often see cars sitting in the parking lot, and he would assume they were detectives because he was still on the run. Looking back, I should have never gotten pregnant by this man after everything he had already put me through—the cheating, never being home, always on the run, and already having children by two different women. That was my first child.

We moved not too far from that apartment, and that's when I started hearing rumors from different people that he was messing with a woman I'll call *Cookie*. I'm not calling out real names because this book isn't about them—it's about what I went through, how I healed, and how I hope to help someone else.

I turned into an investigator—checking his phone, his pockets, his car, anything I could to find proof. When you have to live like that with someone, the relationship is already broken. I kept hearing about this one woman, but of course he denied it, and I didn't have solid proof.

One day, I found a phone he was hiding and decided to contact her. She covered for him like many women do and claimed she was talking to his cousin—who was actually his friend. I would never lie to another woman for a man, especially one who was lying to me. She knew he had a girlfriend, and she knew exactly who I was. She had seen me one night at a club.

I remember noticing a group of girls turning around and looking at me over and over again, and I felt something wasn't right. When I finally confronted her, it was confirmed. You're messing with my man, yet somehow you have an attitude? I should be the one upset, not you.

Looking back, God always had my back and made sure I found out what this man was doing. I truly believe God was saying, *I've shown you enough—you just keep choosing to stay.* And sadly, I did. Twenty-three years later, I finally walked away. That's hard to admit.

Yes, it speaks volumes about their character—but we also have to take accountability for ourselves. At the end of the day, I was the one who stayed and kept accepting the pain. There came a point when I had to admit that I stayed too long.

One day, while he was asleep, I searched his pockets, took his keys, and went through his car looking for proof. He had a Dodge Magnum at the time. I had a gut feeling he was cheating, and too many people were telling me the same thing—including his ex. She genuinely seemed concerned about me. Maybe a part of her was happy he was cheating on me, since I was the woman, he left her for.

But I've learned something important—no one can take a person from you. If they leave, it's because they chose to. A person makes the choice to leave because they want to. Something told me to look under the car hood—my spirit. I had never, ever looked under his hood before. Why would I? I wasn't looking for anything mechanical. But I popped the hood and started looking around, and guess what I found—a cell phone. Who would ever think to look under a car hood for a phone?

I went through the phone and found a text message from Cookie saying she loved him. That's when I called her, and she lied for him. I went back to our apartment, woke him up, and like the manipulator he was, he got madder than I was. He claimed the phone was his cousin's, started fussing and cussing, and completely flipped the script. What we call it now is gaslighting—changing the subject, deflecting, and making himself the victim. Then he left the house.

I was upset and crying because I knew he was lying. Why hide your so-called cousin's phone under the hood of your car? All that anger and defensiveness was just to take the heat off him. This man was a full-blown narcissist. I am so aware of that manipulation tactic now that no man will ever be able to play me like that again. The moment someone starts that behavior, I may just walk away from the entire relationship because trauma has a way of resurfacing. I am not dealing with childless behavior like that. Be a man or a woman and take accountability. If you cheated and you're truly sorry, say it. But when you lie and deflect, you are bound to repeat the same cycle.

If we can't sit down and talk like adults without it blowing up, then there is no need to talk at all.

At that same apartment, another time I searched his pockets and found some keys that were not his car keys. I went outside and pressed the alarm, and it belonged to a small red four-door car parked on the side street near our apartment. I went through that car and found mail with the same girl's name and address—the same girl from the text messages.

Of course, he lied again. He said his cousin was using his car and that he had taken hers. How disrespectful is it to drive another woman's car to our house? And how disrespectful for a woman, knowing he has a girlfriend; to let him use her car knowing he was going home to another woman. Women are still doing this today. Put yourself in her shoes—what if that was you? Would you want to be hurt like that?

He flipped the argument again, as usual, and left. He probably went straight to her house. This man was a compulsive liar and a cheater. I took one of the bills from her car and would randomly drive by her house. One day, I caught him, her, and the cousin sitting on the porch together. I walked up and asked what they were doing. They all lied, saying he was there with the cousin. Just lie after lie.

Eventually, I found out the truth, even though I already felt deep down they were lying the entire time. Those three years while he was on the run were the worst. He didn't care about anything, especially knowing he was eventually going to jail once they caught him. He was clubbing, having fun, cheating, and doing whatever else he wanted.

He finally got caught in December 2007. Our son was almost two at that time. One day, I decided to go see him, but it was a pop-up visit. He didn't know I was coming. I only visited on certain days because I worked and didn't want to go down there every day after work. He was going to court the next day, and I just wanted to surprise him before they decided what they were going to do.

I checked in and stood against the wall, waiting for the group before me to finish their visit. Before the next group of inmates came out for their visit, I heard a familiar voice—one I had heard before. She mentioned a specific date, the exact day he went to jail. I stepped around the corner, and there she was. It was the same girl, Cookie, the one he had been lying about all that time. In that moment, I knew I hadn't been crazy. I had known they were lying.

When he saw me standing there, he looked like he had seen a ghost. I started giving him a piece of my mind, and she got up and walked away. I hurried, trying to catch up with her, but the elevator caught me and my son. I wasn't able to reach her because you have to check out downstairs at the desk, and she left before I did while I was still telling him exactly how I felt.

By the time my son and I made it outside, she was already in her car. She drove past us while talking mess. That moment marked the beginning of the drama between me and her. I knew all along that he was cheating—I just didn't have enough proof because that man was always going to lie. That gut feeling is never wrong.

I wish I had walked away a long time ago. Had I done that, I would never have experienced the pain I went through during this divorce. Staying with a man who continues to show you that he will not change only causes more pain. They don't change until they are ready. It doesn't matter how good of a woman you are—it has nothing to do with you. They have to make the choice to change. We cannot change people. That is between them and God. We are not God.

That was in 2007. It is now 2026. We started dating in 2001, and that man is still operating with the same behavior and character. I finally walked away in September 2024, and our divorce was finalized in November 2024. Now that I had the courage to leave, I can honestly say I am glad I did. I will never take that man back. There is strength in walking away. Yes, it is painful for a little while, but it is nothing compared to a lifetime of continuous pain if I had stayed.

He was sentenced to three and a half years, and once again, I stayed. Me and my son spent long hours driving on highways to see him. Some of those trips were exhausting there and back. I visited him every other weekend the entire time he was incarcerated. I kept money on his books, wrote letters, and accepted calls from him regularly. You would think that after everything I did for him, he would finally do right by me—but he didn't.

He came home in 2011. I got pregnant, and we had our second son in 2012. As always, he talked a good game about doing right this time. And for a few months, he did—mostly because he had a monitor on his leg and couldn't really move around much. He got a job, thanks to my big brother helping him get hired at his company, and he got a car. You would think with a job and a family, there would be no reason to return to the streets.

But when that lifestyle is all, you know since your teenage years, that's what you gravitate back to. The hanging out, cheating, and toxic behavior started immediately.

I don't know what I was thinking, continuing to stay with this man. I was pregnant, and here we go again with the sneaky behavior. I turned back into an investigator. One night, after finding messages in his phone, I spoke to one of the women he had been involved with. When I told her I was pregnant, she claimed she had an abortion. Whether that was true or not, I'll never know.

She told me about a night she went to a club where he was. I'm sure he invited her—it was his friend's club. She said there was a pregnant girl there. That pregnant girl was me. I remember thinking, *you knew it was me—stop playing.*

I told her plainly, I cannot be with a man who is already in a relationship. I want who I'm with to want only me. I refuse to be second to another woman.

And this is why I finally chose myself.

Men cheat partly because there are women who are willing to accept it. Yes, it is the man's behavior and his responsibility, but if no one was willing to be involved in that mess, he would be forced to either be faithful or be alone. We have to set boundaries and stop letting people say or do whatever they want while we just go with the flow. This goes both ways—there are good men out there who deal with bad women, too.

At that time, we were on the same phone plan, so I was able to check his call log and his location. I'm glad I didn't let it consume me to the point where it affected my daily life or sent me into depression, because I endured a lot with this man. Yes, I would get angry and extremely hurt, but I forgave far too much. I had a son and another baby on the way to take care of.

I checked his location so often that it started to become unhealthy. I was pregnant and constantly worried about what he was doing. Eventually, I reached a point where I told myself, *It is what it is.* I stopped checking and stressing over it because I hadn't found anything at that time. Sometimes all you can do is sit back, pray, and let God work. The Bible says there is nothing hidden that will not be revealed.

One day, I was minding my business, watching television, when something in my spirit told me to check the locator. I jumped up, got on the computer, and checked his location. It showed a hotel off the 59 North freeway. Suddenly, the address disappeared. I called his phone, but it was off and went straight to voicemail. He knew that if he turned the phone off, I wouldn't be able to locate him—but I had already seen where the hotel was.

I quickly got dressed, got my son ready, and headed to the hotel. My son was about six years old at the time. When I arrived, his car was backed up directly in front of one of the doors. The parking lot was full, so I had to park a few cars down. Big and pregnant, I got out of the car, left my son inside, and walked over to knock on the door.

He looked out the window but refused to come out. I stood there for a moment, then decided to walk back to my car because he wasn't coming out and my child was still inside. As I got closer to my car, he hit the alarm, ran out, and jumped into his car. I chased him but couldn't catch him, so I threw a stick I had in my hand and hit the back window of his car.

I then knocked on the hotel door and asked the woman inside to open it. She asked if I was going to fight her. I told her no, so she opened the door. I asked her a few questions, and she told me the truth. After that, I left and went home.

What struck me most was the fact that this man left me there, pregnant, not knowing whether that woman would harm me or fight me. I cannot believe I stayed through all of that. It was so long ago that I don't dwell on it now—I forgave him and let it go—but writing this book brings everything back and makes me realize just how much I truly endured with this man.

He was not capable of love. He was deeply damaged by something in his past that caused him to treat women the way he did. I put him out, but not for long, because he came back crying and apologizing, as usual. I had my son shortly after that in 2012.

We were still having problems, but I didn't catch him cheating after that. I was too busy working, taking my sons to football practice, and focusing on being a mother. I kept myself busy and poured everything into my children. It felt like I was a single mother while still in a relationship.

The streets were always his main priority—and they still are to this day. We have a thirteen-year-old son now, and he barely spends time with him. A few years passed, and I finally got tired. In 2015, I left him. I moved out of our apartment and stayed with my nephew for a few months so I could save money and pay off some debt. I stayed there for about six months, then moved back into the same apartment where I had lived before. He went right back to doing what he did best—clubbing and living the street life.

I talked to him for a few months after that, but one day everything changed. I was at my aunt's church, and the message the pastor preached touched my soul. The message was about dealing with a married man. By that time, we had been together fourteen years, yet he had still never divorced his ex-wife. I knew that message was for me. From that moment on, I completely left him alone. Our interactions were strictly about our sons—no sex, no emotional conversations, and no entertaining words without actions.

Later that year, in October 2015, he went back to jail. At that time, we were not talking at all. I had heard he was dealing with another woman. The following year, in 2016, we slowly began talking again when he would call to speak with his children. I started taking the boys to see him, and eventually we developed a friendship. We had healthy conversations, nothing inappropriate.

During that time, I told him I had become more involved in church and had made intentional changes in my life. I stopped watching a lot of television, especially reality and drama shows. I began reading books and spending time in the Bible. I became more active in my church and started volunteering. Interestingly, after recently leaving him for good, I find myself back in that same place—deeply connected to God, almost finished reading the entire Bible, and reading healing and spiritual growth books.

I feel ten times closer to God now, and my faith has increased tremendously. Looking back, I can see that he was a major distraction. All the chaos, arguments, and stress pulled my focus away from God. God had to disrupt that relationship to bring me back into alignment. But this time, there is no going back—ever. I will not repeat that cycle with him.

I love being single while focusing on God. I love my peace and quiet. I am healing and growing from trauma while preparing to be a wife—because I am still a wife. I was just married to the wrong men.

During his last incarceration from 2015 to 2016, we talked about trying again. Once again, he claimed he had changed and knew what he needed to do. That turned out to be another mistake. The boys and I started visiting him more often. At the time, he sounded right and appeared to have a good head on his shoulders.

He came home in August 2016 and got a job, once again thanks to my brother. It was a good company, and he stayed there for about three years—the longest job he had ever held. Before he came home, I set clear boundaries about what I would and would not accept. One of those boundaries was non-negotiable: he had to get a divorce. He was still married to his ex-wife at that time.

He moved quickly to make that happen, although she still gave him problems about signing the papers. He was finally divorced in 2017. I truly believed he had changed—only to find out again that I had been bamboozled.

At first, everything looked good. We were going to church, he wasn't hanging out, and he stayed away from his old crowd. He went to work and came straight home. Life finally felt peaceful. He proposed to me in October 2017 at our son's football game. I was happy, and of course, I said yes.

We set our wedding date for six months later—March 24, 2018, the day after my birthday. Those six months were exhausting. We worked hard and paid for everything ourselves, and we had a beautiful wedding. However, just one week before the wedding, we got into a major argument—all because he didn't want to go to church. That day got bad. The police were called, and his mother and one of his cousins came after he called them. That angry temper came out once again. He refused to give me my keys so we could go to church, and we started tussling right there in front of the boys. I told them to go to their room. That's when I called the police—because he would not give me my keys. All of this happened simply because he didn't want to go to church. Nothing but the devil. If you don't want to go, then just stay home and let us go.

He acted a fool in front of the police, completely ignorant, while his mother kept trying to calm him down. This man is emotionally unstable, always throwing temper tantrums, with no self-control. I thank God that he didn't damage me or my sons during all that chaos. Just like the Bible says, a lack of self-control is the mark of a fool. He was hot-headed and reckless.

When we argued, he would call other family members and start arguments with them for no reason at all. He caused my brother not to be in our wedding. On the day of the wedding, he called my brother at work, cursing him out for absolutely no reason. My brother's name wasn't even mentioned, yet he still went off on him. He would often say hurtful things about my family— "Call your family" during arguments. What does my family have to do with us arguing? Nothing.

This man had two completely different personalities. It always felt like he was dealing with some unresolved trauma. I wanted to call the wedding off so badly, but the thought of canceling everything a week before was embarrassing. Everything was already paid for, and we would have lost so much money. I stayed angry that entire week leading up to the wedding day. Back then, I could hold on to a grudge for a while—thankfully, I've grown past that now.

Eventually, I let it go. All of our family and friends were there, and he seemed happy to be marrying me. We had a good time celebrating, and then we went on our honeymoon with our sons. For a moment, it felt like things might finally be right.

But just a few months later, he went right back to his old ways. Looking back, I believe he behaved just long enough to marry me, then returned to being who he truly was. People don't change just because they do better for a short period of time. This entire marriage—from 2018 until our divorce in 2024—was hard. Yes, there were some good moments, but the bad still outweighed the good.

He went back to hanging in the streets and stopped going to church with his family. That hurt me deeply because we were supposed to be a family, united—especially in faith. How are you supposed to be a man of God, a husband, and a leader if you're not going to church with your family? What are you teaching your sons? That mom goes to church while dad stays behind?

What happened to *a family that prays together stays together*? I know he knows God, but he was never on the same spiritual level that I was. That's when I truly understood the meaning of being equally yoked. Two cannot walk together unless they agree.

The one thing I could say is that cheating was not our main issue during the marriage—at least until the final breakup. Our biggest problems were his constant presence in the streets and his failure to act like a husband and an active father to his sons. To be honest, I don't even know what he was really doing because he was never home. I was busy working, raising our sons, and running my small

T-shirt business. I didn't hang out in the streets, so I couldn't keep track of him.

Eventually, we moved into a townhouse where me and my sons still live today. But the toxicity continued—constant arguing, fussing, and conflict, mainly because he was never home and wasn't fulfilling his responsibilities as a husband. I was managing everything in that household—finances, working, running my business, taking care of the kids, and even handling his business—while he stayed in the streets. I would fuss, curse, and put him out what felt like once a week. It probably wasn't that often, but it felt constant. That behavior was immature on my part, but I was exhausted and sick of his disrespect. He brought out the worst in me. My mouth became foul, and I didn't like the way I talked to him. I had no self-control at times because his behavior was so disrespectful.

I had to work on myself too, because no one should have that much control over you that they can cause you to act out of character. Still, the same cycle continued all the way into 2023, when we had our first separation. That separation lasted about a month before he came back home. He would do better for a week, maybe two, and then fall right back into his old behavior.

Three months later, we separated again, and this time he was gone for almost two months. I filed for divorce, but I canceled it when we got back together at the end of January 2024. I had reached out to him to sign the divorce papers, and then here he came saying he didn't want a divorce—and here I went again, giving in.

Truthfully, I don't believe he really wanted to come back home. He said he wanted to make it work, but his excuse was that I kept putting him out and that he didn't feel like it was his house. So, he came back, but he was distant. I could tell something was off. Yes, I had filed for divorce, but I was still willing to work on the marriage because at that time his main issue was hanging in the streets. Compared to everything else, I saw that as minor and believed we could work through it.

Forgiveness does not mean reconciliation. According to the Bible, that alone wasn't grounds for divorce, so I stayed. But I believe he was cheating again when he came back that last time. There were things I noticed—his behavior was different. When I called him out, he gave excuses that made no sense. Why come back if you were already cheating? I didn't beg him to return—I reached out for him to sign the divorce papers. That was his way out.

But he wanted to have his cake and eat it too. He wanted to keep me because I was a good woman, but he also wanted to do what he wanted—cheat and stay in the streets. He came home just to continue being the same person. I was a woman who loved him, prayed for him, and encouraged him to be better, but he did not encourage or support me the way a husband should. I stayed because I saw his potential and because we had been together for so many years. I kept giving him time to get it together.

About a month after he returned, the arguments started again. He was back in the streets, trying to be "transparent" by telling me what he was doing, asking me to give him a few months and promising he would stop. He knew I wasn't dealing with that life anymore. I was too old for that mess, and I was not about to be running to anybody's jailhouse again. My sons were definitely not going, either. I refused to expose them to that lifestyle.

That is why I was so strict raising my boys—I did not want them turning out like him. He was supposed to be the father figure, but I was both the mother and the father. My sons leaned on me more because I was the one who was consistently there. Dad was rarely home.

By May 2024, things had gotten really bad. We argued constantly. I couldn't say anything about his behavior without him becoming defensive. While living in that townhouse, this was the second time he pulled a gun on me—this time because I told him I wanted a divorce.

Even then, I still didn't believe he would ever truly change. I honestly believed one day he would snap, and I thank God he never did. He started getting mean about everything—anytime I tried to talk to him about his behavior or about fixing our marriage. He would fuss and curse, and I would just look at him. At times, his anger was so intense that he didn't even look like himself—it felt dark, almost evil. I don't care if I ever see that man again.

I truly believe he was behaving that way to force me to leave, because he wasn't man enough to leave on his own. Well, I gave him what he wanted. I had him served and put right out of the house. The old Tanya was gone. I was done putting up with him after twenty-three long years. I may give chances, but I am not weak, and I am not going to beg any man to act right or stay with me. It was time for him to pack his things and go.

Toward the end, something deep inside me knew he was not meant for me. We were moving in two different directions— I was growing spiritually, and he was still living worldly. Everything came to a head the week of June 24, the same week I was planning to go to Cancun. That was the week I found out he was cheating.

That Tuesday, we got into a huge argument. All I did was wake him up a little earlier for work because I wanted to talk about fixing our marriage. He went completely off—fussing and cursing about nothing. I started crying, thinking, *what is happening? I'm just trying to save my marriage.* The old cursing Tanya was gone by then, and all I could do was cry and try to speak calmly. I was fighting for our marriage, but he clearly was not.

My work desk was in our bedroom, and I became so upset that I got up and went into my closet to pray. A little while later, he came into the closet still fussing, cursing, and saying hurtful things. That felt so disrespectful—not just to me, but to God. That was the day I filed for divorce. I said, *oh no, this is devilish behavior.*

I found a lawyer online and paid them that same day. He eventually left for work, and I went back into the closet to pray some more. I said, *Lord, this man has to be doing something to be this angry and hateful toward me.* I believed he was pushing me to put him out so he could go back to the streets, especially since he had recently lost yet another job—something that always seemed to happen.

I prayed, *Lord, if my husband is committing adultery, please expose it. Your Word says nothing hidden will remain concealed.* I went back to my desk to work, and suddenly the word *recorder* dropped into my spirit.

God never let me down. I was the one who kept taking this man back—but not this time.

I remembered that almost ten years earlier, I had purchased a small recorder for a job. I didn't even know if I still had it. I searched everywhere—high and low. To this day, I don't even remember where I found it, but I did.

At the time, he was using my brother's car because his had broken down. He came home early that day acting nice, trying to make up for how ugly he had been earlier. He gave a fake apology and was right back to his old self the very next day.

That next day, I placed the recorder in the car. The following morning, before he woke up for work, I retrieved it. While he was still asleep, I started listening. I heard him in the car with a woman— someone he claimed was just a "friend" and this girl was a friend to me.

I screamed and asked him, *"Are you messing with niece?* That's the name he called her. I knew this girl before I knew him. We used to be close back in the day. She called him her uncle. I should have known something was not right how they always stayed close over the years, but I didn't think he would ever do something like that. He said no and acted like he had no idea what I was talking about, because I hadn't told him how I knew. He was sitting in my brother's car with this girl for over an hour. That's disgusting to me cheating with this girl that everybody knows him as her uncle, but not blood niece. I know what I heard and at some point, the most definitely slept around. It's funny how this rumor came to me a few years prior. He left for work, and I stayed home listening to the entire recording. It stayed in the car with him all day.

And that was when everything finally became clear. That morning, after he left the house, it was clear he had pulled over to pick up another phone—one he was hiding from me again. On the recording, I heard him call a woman named Candy, or Candace, on his way to work. Not his wife—but her. She clearly knew he was married because he was telling her all of my business, including that I was going to Cancun that Friday and that he could come over and "chill" with her while I was gone. He even said, *"At least I won't have to hear her mouth while she's gone."*

He was talking mess about me, lying about who I was and why I confronted him so much. He never told the truth—that I fussed because he wasn't acting like a husband or a father, always in the streets and never home. If you're going to talk down on your wife, at least tell the truth. It's funny how the cheating spouse creates a false narrative to make themselves look good, while the other person doesn't even realize *they* are the problem in the relationship.

He even called her—or possibly another woman—on his lunch break. This man was truly living a double life. On the same recording, I heard him talking to one of his homeboys about street business. He mentioned having another place—some type of spot he was using. At that moment, I realized I didn't even know who this man was anymore. He was a compulsive liar, living a completely separate life behind my back.

Nothing got better after that. At that point, I was just waiting on the lawyer to move forward with the divorce. I went to Cancun that week, and he even dropped me off at the airport. I tried my best to hold it together on that trip, but it was one of the hardest weeks of that entire year. I enjoyed time with my family and friends, but I kept retreating to my room to cry. I had to keep calling my close friend just to get through it. I tried not to cry too much so my family wouldn't notice, but the dark circles under my eyes showed the lack of sleep and the emotional exhaustion.

When I came back home, we talked again. That's when he started fake crying and acting like he wanted to kill himself. He went into our closet with a gun, and I immediately ran into my oldest son's room and called my friend. I was terrified. I didn't want to hear a gunshot or walk in on something that would traumatize me for the rest of my life. No matter how bad our marriage was, I didn't want him dead.

We talked, and once again, I tried to make it work. He claimed he had just met that girl at a gas station and that it meant nothing. He agreed to get Life360 so I could see his whereabouts at all times. But nothing actually changed. He was still hanging out, still sneaking, still behaving the same way. The only difference was the app.

Eventually, I got tired and deleted him from Life360. He immediately called, going off, accusing *me* of doing something. Meanwhile, I was always at home with our kids. The liar always deflects.

In August, we took our son to college. When we came back, he got a text saying he had been fired again. Every job this man ever had, he lost—always because of his lack of work ethic. He even admitted that he could make more money in the streets. Yet he would get offended when I said he had a street mentality. The truth hurt him.

I was exhausted—tired of him losing jobs, not being home, cheating, and on top of all that, being cruel to me. Two weeks before he was served with divorce papers, I sent him one final long text explaining his behavior and how it had affected me. After that, I stopped talking. I didn't say another word.

When a woman gets tired, there is nothing you can say or do to change her mind. And I was there. I deserved better than that man. The only reason I stayed so long was because of our history and my hope that he would change. But in the process, I was losing myself.

And this time, I chose me. I eventually reached a point where I had to stop wearing myself down. I started having medical issues— nothing life-threatening, but problems that were most likely caused by years of constant stress. I ended up needing two procedures to correct some issues and one major surgery. I am good now, thank God. All that yelling, arguing, and emotional turmoil truly takes a toll on your body.

Ironically, I had one of those procedures done on the same day he was served with divorce papers. When I sent him that long message, I immediately called my lawyer and told him I wanted him served as soon as possible. When I stopped speaking to him, he stopped speaking too, and he continued coming and going as he pleased. It took everything in me not to turn back into the old Tanya—to curse him out and tell him to get out of my house immediately.

But I knew if I did that, it could cause issues with serving him, depending on where he was staying, and that would delay the divorce and cost me more money. I wanted out. His time was long overdue. I stayed and tolerated his mess far too long. I should have left that unstable narcissist years ago. I used to get angry when calling him that because this was someone I once loved deeply and planned to spend my life with.

When I took him back before we got married, I genuinely left all the past behind. I wasn't replaying those moments in my head—I truly moved on. But writing this book has forced me to relive that trauma, and at times it almost makes me feel like I could hate him. But I don't. The Bible says to pray for your enemies. We share children together, and I don't wish harm on him.

When I started my healing process, I began journaling and reflecting on my relationships. That's when all these memories resurfaced—not to hurt me, but to help me heal correctly and to understand what it was in me that kept forgiving men like this so I wouldn't repeat the cycle a third time. The only conclusion I could come to was that I have a forgiving heart. That does not mean I am weak. Not at all—and both men knew that.

I remember one of them saying early on that he liked how feisty I was. Never again. Walking away after being with someone for so many years was hard, but I learned that years mean nothing if they are filled with pain. Staying caused far more damage than leaving ever did.

I am still in my healing journey, but the pain is gone. The uncontrollable crying has stopped. I can't say I would go back and change things, because then I wouldn't have my sons—and I wouldn't trade them for anything in the world. I do, however, wish I had left after catching him at that hotel. That should have been the final straw. By then, I already had both of my sons.

Sometimes I wonder what my life would look like if I had left earlier. But I believe God was always with me. That's why I was able to uncover the truth so many times without even searching—led by my spirit. I believe all things work together for those who love God. This was part of a bigger plan, maybe even to write this book and share my testimony to help someone else.

I never imagined I'd write a book—not in a million years. As I write this, it has been almost two years since we separated and divorced. I have never been happier or more at peace. I set firm boundaries with him. He is blocked on everything. I don't see him, and I don't want to. I don't care if I never see him again.

This man put me through so much. What kind of person wrongs someone who did nothing but love and support them? He will have to live with the truth that I never did anything to him. God is a just God. I don't seek revenge—the Bible says vengeance belongs to the Lord, and He will repay. I pray for him because he is still the father of my sons, and I forgive him because my peace depends on it.

I am not bitter about what he did. I have chosen peace. This time, I am waiting on God for my spouse. He is not here yet, but I already pray for him. I am not desperate, and I am not searching. I am focused on God and working toward the goals He has placed in my heart.

Like Ruth, I am working. And while I am working, God will send my Boaz—when I am not expecting it. Until then, I am preparing myself to be an even better wife: healed, whole, discerning, and grounded in faith.

I thank God every day for getting me out of that marriage. But right after it happened, I didn't understand it at all. All I felt was the pain. It's been a year and a half now, and so much truth has been coming to light about this narcissistic man I was with. I just recently found out he's cheating with his cousin's baby mama. What's crazy is, years ago at his cousin's wedding, I felt something wasn't right about her. That same girl is married, yet here they are. Neither of them honor God with that adulterous behavior. Clearly, he doesn't honor married if he cheated on me. It disgusts me. He is a lustful, deceitful man, and I'm still trying to wrap my head around how I didn't fully see it back then. I wanted to believe the good in him so badly, but the truth is, he was moving like a snake the whole time.

There are even more things I've heard—things I won't repeat because I would never betray someone else's trust—but it only confirmed what I now see clearly. This was a man I spent 23 years with, the father of my sons, and now I can barely recognize who he really was. It makes me almost afraid to trust again, because people can pretend to be someone, they're not for years. But even in all of that, I am grateful. God saw what I couldn't see. He protected me in ways I didn't understand at the time and redirected my life before things got even worse. And for that, I will always thank Him for getting me out.

As for that man, his role in my life is complete—just like this chapter.

And that is where his story ends.

He Got Served

He had no idea what was about to hit him.

I was beyond tired, and I didn't want to kick him out before he was served with divorce papers. Months earlier, I had told him I filed for divorce, but when we tried to make things work, he assumed I had canceled it. I hadn't. Something told me not to fully cancel it—just to put it on hold. That decision saved me thousands of dollars and turned out to be the right one, because he did exactly what he always did.

I followed my first mind.

I was off that Friday and the day before because I had a medical procedure done on Thursday. That night, I chose to sleep in my oldest son's room. I didn't even want to sleep next to him. He tried to convince me to come back to bed, but I told him no.

The next morning, I woke up, went downstairs, made my coffee, and sat on the couch watching the news. I was nervous—terrified, actually. He had no idea what was coming. I never told him I was moving forward with the divorce.

I received a text from the process server saying she was on her way. My heart started racing. Not much time passed before there was a knock at the door. I jumped up and answered it. My eyes widened when she asked, "Is John Doe here?"

I said, "Give me one minute."

I went upstairs, woke him up, and told him there was someone at the door for him. He asked who it was, and I said I didn't know. If I had told him, it was a server, he wouldn't have gone downstairs, and the entire purpose would have been defeated.

I went back downstairs and sat on the couch, pretending to watch television. My heart felt like it was beating out of my chest. He came down, opened the door, and the woman asked, "Are you John Doe?"

He said yes.

She replied, "You are being served with divorce papers."

He slammed the door.

Thankfully, she had already confirmed his identity and was able to throw the papers inside before the door shut. If she hadn't, I might still be married today—just like he had been with his first wife for years before I forced him to divorce her. Back then, that was one of my non-negotiables before we got married. By that point, we had already been together for fourteen years, and he was still legally married.

But back to this moment.

He ran upstairs, grabbed a gun, and ran outside after the server.

Thank God she was already gone.

She was just doing her job, and he was so hot-headed and ignorant that I believe he would have hurt her had she still been there. His ego was bruised, but instead of reflecting, he reacted with rage—after months of treating me cruelly while I tried to save our marriage.

I guess he thought I would continue tolerating that behavior.

No.

Eventually, he came back inside when he realized the server was gone. He grabbed only a few items of clothing. I calmly asked him to take more and told him I'd give him time to come back for the rest. That was a mistake.

He exploded—calling me out of my name and yelling, "You're going to die today!"

I lost it. I cursed him out right back. I had just had a procedure the day before and wasn't supposed to get worked up, but he pushed me past my limit.

He called his mother, cursing and disrespecting me while she was on the phone. She defended me, and that made him even angrier. He accused her of always taking up for me and called me vile names. He was furious.

The server texted me asking if I was okay and told me she had called the police because she saw him chase her with a gun. When the police arrived, he was still there. They tried to calm both of us down, because we were both yelling.

I knew I looked foolish arguing with him—but Proverbs says, *"Never argue with a fool; onlookers won't be able to tell the difference."* That moment humbled me deeply.

Your spouse is not supposed to bring out the worst in you, and he absolutely did.

I had felt long before that he was not meant for me. I was trying to live a godly life, and he was living worldly. *"Two cannot walk together unless they agree."* We weren't walking together at all.

The police said they couldn't force him to leave since we were married and this was his residence, but he eventually left on his own. One officer asked how long we had been together. When I said twenty-three years, he said that was a long time to let go.

It is—but not when infidelity and abuse are involved.

I'm actually glad now that it was someone I knew—a woman he referred to as his "niece." Had it been a stranger, I might have forgiven him again. But this was different. She knew me. That level of betrayal woke me up.

Thankfully, our youngest son was at school, and our oldest had just started college. My boys were disappointed when I explained we were divorcing, but they understood. He had barely been present anyway. Their world had always been built around Mom.

After everyone left, I sat quietly until my youngest came home. My lawyer called to check on me after hearing what happened. He said he planned to pursue a restraining order.

His brother and sister even called to check on me. They knew his temper. They had seen it before.

The following days were quiet. I went to church that Sunday and felt peace I hadn't felt in years. On Monday, his mother finally called, telling me about the difficulties she had endured with her children's father. My lawyer later notified me of our court date: October 1, 2024.

He didn't show up.

That delayed everything, but the divorce process continued. I barely made it to court that day; the judge was calling my name as I walked in.

He came by later to pick up belongings and had the nerve to accuse me of trying to get him arrested. Still no accountability.

Two weeks later, the emotions finally hit me. I journaled everything. October 2, 2024, was the first day I felt truly heavy.

That same day, he texted me: *"I love you forever, Tanya."*

The divorce became final right before Thanksgiving, though I didn't receive confirmation from my lawyer until December 3, 2024. My heart dropped when I saw the email.

In March, on what would have been our eighth anniversary, he texted me "Happy Anniversary." I don't know what he was thinking.

Divorce is one of the hardest things a person can endure. I wouldn't wish it on anyone. Marriage is a sacred covenant; one I honor deeply.

I don't regret my sons. They are my greatest blessing. What I went through made me stronger, sharper, and closer to God.

I didn't understand during the pain—but now I see it.

All things truly worked together for my good.

I'm at peace now. I'm happy. I'm healed. My skin is glowing. My heart is clear.

God knows my heart.

I'm not perfect—but He is forgiving.

The Painful Aftershock

The pain didn't come immediately after he left the house that day. I think it hit about two weeks later. At first, I was still angry—angry about how he cursed me out, especially on the phone with his mother, and in front of the police officers. You chose to disrespect your wife because I finally got tired of your behavior. When I stood in front of the judge two weeks later, I was extremely nervous. I was hoping she would grant the divorce that day, but it was too soon. Legally, he had to be given time.

It was the very next day when my emotions fully hit me. That same day, he came by the house to get some of his belongings. Maybe seeing him set me back—I'm not completely sure—but that was the day everything came crashing down. That's also when I started journaling my feelings and emotions consistently. I've journaled on and off since I was a teenager, but maybe all of that was leading me to this moment in my life—writing this book.

I never imagined I would be an author. I never even considered writing a book until last year, after the heartbreak.

The pain was so deep it felt like there was a literal hole in my heart. I cried uncontrollably. I couldn't sleep. Dark circles formed under my eyes, and I lost almost thirty pounds. Over the years, I become comfortable and let myself go while with him, gaining weight. Looking at myself now feels like déjà vu—similar to how my life shifted back in 2015 when I first left him.

Back then, just like now, I grew closer to God. I stopped watching so much television, started reading books, and spent long periods sitting in my room in peace and quiet. My oldest son was about nine years old then and would say, "Mom, all you do is sit in this room." But the truth is, I was at peace—then and now—each time I walked away from him.

As time passed, the pain intensified. I thank God I was working from home during that season because I cried day after day. I began having eye issues, likely from crying so much—they felt dry and painful. My oldest son was away at college, and thankfully, my youngest was in school during the day. Still, dealing with heartbreak while trying to keep a straight face for your children is brutal.

Some days, when my youngest was home, I would retreat into my closet to cry. My closet is inside my restroom, so I would close the bathroom door and cry quietly so he wouldn't see me. One day, during a conversation, he told me he had seen me crying in the closet. I thought to myself—what kind of man hurts his wife so deeply while she is raising his children?

To this day, I don't think he truly understands how badly he hurt me—or maybe he doesn't care. Either way, I would be a fool to ever let him back after the way he played in my face during that final season. There's nothing he could say to undo that level of damage.

I remember looking at our wedding photos, crying, and slipping my wedding ring back on, still hoping he would change—even after everything. You don't realize how toxic an environment is until you step out of it and truly reflect. I had become so immune to the constant arguing, gaslighting, lack of accountability, and chaos that I was clinging to hope instead of reality.

Now, writing this book and seeing all the toxicity laid out clearly, I know I will never allow myself to go through that again. I'm very intentional now about guarding my heart (*Proverbs 4:23*). I spent many nights crying and praying in that closet—it became my war room. That heartbreak was positioning me for my greatest victory—finding myself again.

I sought the Lord, and He heard my cry. At times, though, I grew frustrated. I would pray and feel like God wasn't listening. I wanted to hear His voice, that still small whisper everyone talks about. I had questions—*Why me? What did I do wrong?* There were moments I even wondered if God was punishing me for past mistakes.

But I had asked God for forgiveness when I learned better. This had nothing to do with punishment—it was about exposure. It was about fruit. He was the bad tree.

One day, while babysitting my great-niece, I sat at my desk doing everything I could to keep from crying. That's one of the hardest things—holding back tears when you're around others. Journaling and talking to God became my lifeline. I felt like I didn't have anyone I could be completely vulnerable with. I was always the one counseling others, helping everyone else—but who was there for me?

Eventually, I opened up to close family members. They supported me, but they didn't see the depth of my pain. Only God truly knows how much it hurt. My nephew sent flowers to my home, and the message on the card broke me—in a good way. My mom and sister checked in on me often.

The pain was so intense that I sometimes felt tempted to jump into another relationship just so someone could take the pain away. But that's how I ended up here in the first place—jumping from one relationship to the next without healing. I knew better this time.

Slow songs would play, and I would cry like a child—deep, uncontrollable sobbing. The kind of crying you do when you're completely broken. Nights were the hardest. After twenty-three years with someone, the silence is loud when they're gone. That loss hits deep.

I can't remember exactly when the pain lifted or how long it lasted—but I know the hardest part is over. Do I still cry sometimes? Of course. But those tears are no longer about missing him. They come from gratitude—thinking about how God brought me through.

Now, when I cry, they're happy tears.

I had to set boundaries with family and friends—asking them not to share information about him or speak his name, especially regarding the woman he cheated with. Boundaries are necessary during healing. I needed peace to fully detach.

One day he even texted me saying, *"It looks like everything is fine on the outside, but it's eating me up on the inside."* I was confused. How are you hurting over something you caused? That kind of thinking showed how broken he truly was.

I believe in doing unto others as you would have them do unto you. I care deeply about people's feelings, and I would never intentionally hurt someone. Every time I left him, I ran to God. And this time, my relationship with God is stronger than ever.

He almost broke me—but he didn't.

Even after betrayal and isolation, God restored me. I found my confidence again, and He will do the same for you. This season did not expose my weakness—it revealed my strength. Something around me may have broken, but *I* did not break.

I cried—but I didn't quit.

Survival itself is proof of my assignment.

It's been over a year and a half since the divorce, and I am doing just fine. I forgave him. I forgave her. I didn't seek revenge—*Romans 12:19* reminds us that vengeance belongs to the Lord.

God is a just God. He saw everything.

Even when I couldn't speak through the tears, God was there. *Weeping may endure for a night, but joy comes in the morning.* If you are walking through heartbreak, lean on God's promises. He is close to the brokenhearted and saves those crushed in spirit.

God allows disruptions to correct direction.

My vision is clear now.

I didn't grow to go back.

I did not grow to go back.

As I was coming out, the enemy didn't want me to leave—but God closed that door. My future is in front of me, not behind me.

Betrayal From the People I Loved

How do you say you love someone and then betray them?

A husband. A friend. People you trusted—people you would have done anything for. People who knew your deepest secrets, your fears, your heart. Three people I loved betrayed me in ways that left a pain so deep it felt unbearable.

I never imagined that a friend I trusted would one day sleep with my boyfriend. He was just as guilty as she was. And then my husband—the man I stood before God with and took vows to—would later betray me as well. With him, I had already seen signs long before we were married, but I chose to give him the benefit of the doubt. He claimed he had changed before we got married, and for a short time, he did. But eventually, he went right back to who he truly was.

What they did to me had nothing to do with me. It had everything to do with their character.

I remember the day I found out about my friend. Some things never leave you. Traumatic moments don't disappear—they just settle quietly in the back of your mind. What hurt most was finding out that everyone seemed to know but me. Her own cousin was the one who told me.

I was angry—beyond angry. I went to her house and, without even fully realizing what I was doing, I broke her window with my fist while yelling for her to come outside. We fought that day, but people stopped us because they didn't want to see two friends fighting like that. I stopped talking to her immediately. What kind of friend does something like that?

I can't even remember what I said to him or whether we broke up then. Shockingly, we stayed together for years after that—and eventually got married. I've seen this pattern happen so often: women pour all their anger onto the other woman and give the man another chance. I wasn't mad at her just because she was a woman—I was mad because she was my friend.

But if I stopped talking to her, I should have stopped talking to him too. He wasn't better than her. That wasn't even the first time he had cheated on me, and it should have been my final straw. Instead, it became part of a pattern.

Later I found out that her own boyfriend had cheated on her and that she was trying to get revenge. But why choose *your friend's* boyfriend? Eventually, years later, I forgave her. What was the point in holding on to that anger when I wasn't with him anymore? We are called to forgive—even when betrayal cuts deeply.

There were only four of us who were truly close back then. Years later, we even went on a cruise together. I'm still close with some of her cousins, including the one who told me the truth. But that experience changed me forever. I'm extremely selective about who has access to me now. Everybody doesn't deserve to be in my circle.

I'm careful with friendships. I'm even more careful about the next man who enters my life. Being betrayed so many times by people I loved made me cautious—sometimes even afraid to trust. But God has not given us a spirit of fear. What He gives us is discernment.

I desire friends who are prayer warriors—friends who will go to God on my behalf. Friends like those in the Bible who tore the roof off just to get their friend to Jesus (Luke 5:18–20). I want friends who love the way I love.

I don't understand how a conscience doesn't convict people when they betray someone. How do you sit in someone's face, laugh, hug them, and feel no conviction after hurting them so deeply? That is diabolical.

Even after learning the truth, both of them continued to show up around me like nothing had happened.

Years later, I still married that man—the same man who slept with my friend. And eventually, he received his consequences when I finally got tired of his cheating and left him for what would become my second betrayal. I went from one broken situation straight into another—same lies, same cheating, just a different body.

I married the same type of man twice.

My second husband caused the deepest pain of all. I should have never married him after everything he had already put me through. We expect betrayal from strangers—but not from those who swear they love us.

I remember crying and begging God to take the pain away. I don't believe he truly understands the pain he caused me—or perhaps he simply doesn't care. Looking back, he never showed real emotional depth during our marriage. He was emotionally unstable, and repeated betrayals made me question everything—his intentions, his capacity to love, and the truth of our entire relationship.

I once read something that said, *"Who a person is at the end of the relationship is who they truly were."* I believe that now. At times, he was so angry, so cruel, that he barely resembled a human being. Living with him meant living in survival mode—monitoring phones, watching behavior shifts, staying alert at all times.

Multiple betrayals change you. They changed me—for the better.

There will be no more second chances. No more forgiving easily. Cheating is a choice, and it takes too much effort to be accidental. I will never accept infidelity again. One time—and that's it.

Healing from repeated betrayal was not instant. It came slowly, painfully, and honestly. I had to grieve the man I thought he could be, the marriage I wanted, and the version of myself who kept surviving instead of living.

Forgiveness does not mean tolerating repeated disrespect. Loyalty cannot be one-sided.

God didn't expose the betrayals to shame me—He exposed them to free me. I was never meant to stay in a place where my dignity was repeatedly violated. I stayed because I hoped he would change. He never did. When something becomes a pattern, it's time to walk away.

God removed me from that marriage at the right time—because staying any longer would have cost me myself.

Even after betrayal and isolation, God restored me. I found my confidence again. What this season revealed was not my weakness—it revealed my strength. Something around me may have broken, but *I* did not break.

I cried—but I didn't quit.

Survival is proof of my assignment.

It has been over a year and a half since my divorce, and I'm doing well. I forgave him. I forgave her—not because they deserved it, but because I refused to let bitterness poison my heart. Forgiveness was for me.

I sought no revenge. Romans 12:19 reminds us that vengeance belongs to the Lord.

God saw everything.

Even when I couldn't speak through my tears, He was there. *Weeping may endure for a night, but joy comes in the morning.* God is close to the brokenhearted and saves those crushed in spirit. Sometimes He allows disruption to correct direction.

My vision is clear now.

I didn't grow to go back.

I did not grow to go back.

As I was coming out, the enemy tried to pull me backward—but God closed the door. My future is in front of me, not behind me.

This betrayal violated my trust in cycles—but it did not destroy me. The pain refined me. What hurt me taught me.

This chapter was painful to write, and it brought me to tears—but it was necessary. Healing happens when truth is told.

My truth is this:

I was faithful.

I was loyal.

I was loving.

And I survived what tried to break me.

In My Waiting Season

This is my waiting season—and it is not empty, it is sacred. This is where my healing truly began. It's the season I kept trying to rush through, but God slowed me down. He peeled back the layers and required me to sit with my broken pieces and trust His hands with the parts of me I didn't know how to fix.

This season is teaching me discernment, patience, and self-worth. God is not withholding love from me—He is preparing me. While my heart is being healed and restored, He is doing a deep work within me. After my second heartbreak, this became my season of surrender and learning to fully trust God.

His Word says He will never leave me nor forsake me. He is close to the brokenhearted and saves those who are crushed in spirit. He saved me—and He will save you too. During that time, He was all that I had, and truly, He was all that I needed.

One day, I looked back and realized the pain was gone. I'm learning to pause, to stop rushing, to stop hiding, and to heal while God does the deep work in me—before sending me the man He has ordained for me.

My desire is to be married again, and I believe God is going to blow my mind with this next—and final—husband. But while I wait, I am preparing myself to be a wife and healing from the trauma of past relationships. Yes, I have had two failed marriages, but that does not define me. I was married to the wrong men. I do not think less of myself because I have been married twice.

I have always been a wife at heart. I wanted to be a wife from a young age, and I believe that is something God placed inside of me. Still, I had work to do within myself.

While my marriages ended because of the men I was with, there were times I was not the wife the Bible describes. We are quick to examine what others did to us, but sometimes we forget to look within. Scripture tells us to remove the speck from our own eye.

Was I a good wife? Yes. Did I make mistakes? Absolutely. A wife is called to honor and respect her husband, and when I was angry and hurt, my mouth became ugly and disrespectful. I kicked him out often, spoke harshly, and said things I should not have said. Looking back, I can see how damaging words can be.

A woman of God does not speak that way. I was still immature in some areas and had growing to do. Now, when I hear other women speak disrespectfully to their husbands, it sounds different to me—because growth changes your perspective.

I am praying to be a wife of noble character.

I am not rushed, and I am not desperate. When the time is right, the Lord will make it happen. I believe that when I am fully healed and prepared, my husband will come unexpectedly—just like Boaz came to Ruth while she was working.

Right now, my focus is God. He is my husband in this season. I do not want distractions. So many people jump from one relationship to the next without healing and end up repeating the same patterns. I did that once—going from my first husband straight into my second, with no healing in between. I married the same man in a different body.

Had I not paused to heal, I believe I would have repeated that cycle a third time. I am so grateful I chose to wait.

The pain was heavy. I wanted someone else to take it away—but God didn't allow that. I didn't understand at the time, but now I do. I had to sit in that pain. I cried. I begged God to take it away. And through that process, He healed me.

During this season, I do not have a side piece, a companion, or anything filling the space. This time is strictly for me and God. After being in a relationship for twenty-three years, healing takes time. You don't just move on—I know I can't.

There are moments I feel ready for love again, but there is also caution—and that's understandable. God has not given us a spirit of fear, but after betrayal, anyone would be careful. Your own spouse—someone you vowed to—sleeping with your friend changes you.

These days, trust feels rare. People often come with agendas. That's why I want my relationship with God stronger than ever before I even think about another relationship. At this stage in my life, I don't have time for games, lies, or cheating. I've already endured enough.

My boundaries are firm now. At the first sign of lying, manipulation, or games—I'm out. I am content being alone until the right time. Too many people accept anything because they fear being alone, but people will only do what you allow.

In this waiting season, God is not only preparing me—He is also preparing my husband. I pray that my discernment continues to sharpen, my wounds are fully healed, and I learn to love myself the way God loves me.

His delays are not denials. They are protection.

His timing is intentional.

Wait on the Lord, and He will renew your strength.

Fighting Battles I Was Never Called to Fight

There is a price that comes with dealing with a married man.

What I thought was love turned into a battlefield—filled with unresolved ties, lingering attachments, and constant drama. God will never have His hand on a relationship that is created while another covenant is still intact. It is never okay to date a married person, even if they claim they are separated. A covenant is still a covenant until it is legally and spiritually dissolved.

I had to learn this the hard way.

I entered a relationship with a married man while I was still married myself, and I paid deeply for that choice. If a man can leave his pregnant wife with a small child, he will most definitely do it to you. During that relationship, I saw exactly who he was.

I do not believe the phrase *"once a cheater, always a cheater"* applies to everyone. People can grow, mature, and change. I cheated and left my first husband when I was in my early twenties—not making an excuse, but at twenty years old, I did not understand marriage. Today, I honor God first. I would never cheat—married or not. Growth matters.

But a grown woman should never desire another woman's husband.

Adultery is a hard **no** for me.

I paid a heavy price for being involved with this married man. I had to deal with his ex-wife and my ex-husband at the same time. She blamed me for everything, and while I understand her pain now, she directed her anger toward the wrong person. He was her husband—not me.

That was my first experience with what people now call "baby mama drama." I did not have drama in my life before this, and I absolutely did not want it in my relationship. I did not have children at that time, and looking back, I wish someone had told me never to date a man with children when you don't have any yourself. Loving kids wasn't the issue—the *complications* were.

I would never chase, harass, or stalk a man who chose to leave me. I would be hurt, yes—but I would not lose my dignity. If someone can leave their spouse for you, that is a red flag. If they claim the relationship is bad but refuse to leave, they are usually the problem.

This relationship began in 2001. We started talking and spending time together, and not once did he tell me he was married. I didn't even think to ask. I found out months later through a cousin of mine who worked with his wife. We were supposed to hang out that day, and when I mentioned his name, she said, *"His wife works with me."* That's how I found out.

When I confronted him later that night, he told me he was only staying until she had the baby—and claimed he wasn't even sure the baby was his. That lie alone should have been enough for me to walk away. Clearly, his wife had no idea he planned to leave.

What kind of man leaves his pregnant wife with a small child?

The very man who later betrayed me.

Soon after, the drama exploded. One day, a pregnant woman and an older woman—around my mother's age—came to my home. It turned out to be his wife and his mother. That was the day I learned she was pregnant. His mother was understandably upset and said, *"My son is cheating right down the street from his home."* We lived just a few apartments away from each other.

I was respectful to both women, but that didn't stop the harassment. After she had the baby, the drama intensified. She began calling my phone constantly, showing up at my home, and following us. My ex-husband was doing similar things, though he eventually stopped. She did not.

Her hurt turned into bitterness—and I became the target.

At one point, she showed up at my house again, claiming she had the right because her husband was there. When she walked away, I let anger take over and kicked her from behind. She almost fell down the cement stairs. Thank God, she caught herself. Had she fallen, one of us could have been dead—and all over a lying man.

That moment changed me.

She later bit me so hard during another altercation that I had to get a tetanus shot. I still have the scar to this day. That was never who I was—but chaos like that changes people. I stayed to myself then, just like I do now. You have to push me very far for me to fight.

The drama continued for years. One night, after repeated harassment, I let anger take over and went to her house following phone calls from her and her friends. That was one of the most dangerous decisions I ever made. Never go to someone else's house angry—you can lose your life behind pride.

She came to the door with a butcher knife.

That night, one of us could have died. Kids were standing in the doorway watching grown adults act recklessly over a man who would eventually betray both of us. I walked away from that realizing how dangerous unhealed anger can be.

This man brought chaos into my life from the very beginning. Just like he hurt his wife to be with me, he later hurt me in the end.

When covenant lines are blurred, confusion becomes the norm.

I fought battles I never signed up for.

God does not bless relationships that require constant emotional warfare. He will never place His approval on unions built on overlap or unresolved bonds. This man never dealt with his past, and both women paid the price.

Healing requires closure.

New beginnings require clean foundations.

The purpose of this chapter is not to bash another woman, but to warn, to heal, and to help others recognize the danger of entering relationships built on broken covenants.

Love yourself enough to walk away.

If someone cheats on their spouse, they will likely cheat on you.

I cannot control other people's wounds, insecurities, or intentions—but I can control my response. My sons deserve peace. I deserve peace.

I am not the option—I am the only one.

I no longer fight battles I was never called to fight.

Healing Journey – My Testimony

This is my healing journey—after betrayal, survival, and the rediscovery of self-worth. I am sharing my story not to glorify my past, but to magnify God's mercy. I share it because I know what it feels like to be tangled in relationships that drain your peace and confuse your spirit. I know what it feels like to carry baggage that was never yours to carry.

I pray that God gives you the strength to walk away from any situation that is stealing your peace. He did it for me, and He will do it for you. In our weakness, God's strength is revealed and made perfect. I will never again accept less than what I deserve—and neither should you.

I forgave too quickly and moved on too fast, becoming so immune to toxic behavior that it began to feel normal. I lived "going with the flow" in chaos, overlooking major red flags—guns being pulled on me, emotionally unstable men, and constant infidelity. I saw the signs, but I ignored them, telling myself, *He would never really do something like that,* or *It's just his temper.*

We see it every day—spouses and partners harming or killing one another because anger and emotions spiral out of control. Overlooking red flags and excusing emotional instability could have cost me my life. I thank God that I am still here to tell my story.

Years later, my first husband admitted that the day he pulled me and my new boyfriend over, his plan was to kill us. He had a gun, and I was terrified. Even though he had wronged me before I left, I had still been his wife. Some people believe they can hurt you over and over again and that you will always stay because you already endured so much. But eventually, a person gets tired.

I thank God that the hardest part is behind me now. Writing this book—reliving the pain—has been the final release of my healing. Before I started writing, there was still a small shattered place in my heart. With every page, I felt that brokenness being lifted. I cried while writing, reopening wounds I had buried, but with each chapter, I exhaled more pain.

There is always purpose in pain. And perhaps God's purpose was for me to share my testimony in this book.

It was difficult to imagine life without the man I had been with for twenty-three years—half of my life. We shared children, which creates a bond that doesn't simply disappear. Looking back, I have asked myself why I stayed in such a toxic relationship for so long. I had become immune to chaos. Only after leaving did, I realize how much turmoil had surrounded my life.

I am setting boundaries now—and I am not bending them. For a time, we were still communicating. It felt like we were still connected—until I made the decision to cut him off completely. I blocked him everywhere for my peace and my healing. My sons are grown; they can communicate with their father directly. There is nothing left for me to say to him, especially after the way he treated me at the end of our marriage.

He must live with the truth that I never did anything to him.

I am the kind of woman he will never encounter again.

I had to choose myself so I could truly heal and leave the past where it belongs. He did what was best for him, without regard for my feelings. If I were the woman I am today, I would have walked away long ago—but everything happens for a reason.

I have grown immensely—biblically and spiritually. No man will ever have the chance to play with my heart again. I now understand how to recognize a person by their fruit. Within three years of my final relationship, I began to see the pattern clearly—twenty years of poor character out of a twenty-three-year relationship. I married and had children with someone who consistently showed me who he was.

For most of that time, I was essentially a single mother. I am proud of how I was raised and how I raised my sons. I was strict because I did not want them to follow the same path as their father—and it paid off. My boys are respectful, disciplined, and grounded. I raised them in the church and established a strong foundation early on.

My youngest is entering high school, and my oldest is going into his junior year at Texas Tech University. I am incredibly proud.

I forgave their father because forgiveness is the godly thing to do—and because he is still their father. I pray he gets his life together for the sake of his children and future grandchildren.

This chapter of my life is closed.

This book represents the ending of one chapter and the beginning of another. Where God is taking me, not everyone is allowed access. His betrayal was part of a bigger plan—he simply played his role. My spiritual maturity chose obedience over revenge, silence over confrontation.

This book gave me the closure I needed.

There is nothing he can say or do that would ever bring me back. My pain had a purpose. I am becoming whole—healed, restored, and still growing. Scripture tells us to put our trust in God, not in people. God will never fail us.

I am not looking back at what I had to leave behind—begging God to remove pain. My future is ahead of me, with God going before me, making every crooked path straight.

If sharing my story leads even one person to God, then it was worth it.

The peace and joy I have now—only God could have given it to me. I love my quiet home, free from chaos and arguing. My closet has become my sanctuary—the place where I speak to God. I remember lying on that closet floor crying so my son wouldn't see me broken. Holding myself together just to keep him protected was one of the hardest things I've ever done.

One day my son said, *"Mom, I saw you in the closet crying."* That broke me—but it also reminded me how much healing I truly needed.

I am grateful that season is behind me.

I have my confidence back. I can finally see myself without him. This was not my end—this was the end of a painful chapter.

God is up to something. I can feel it, and I trust Him.

Old things have passed away, and behold, all things are becoming new.

I no longer cry uncontrollably, begging God to take the pain away. When I cry now, they are tears of gratitude—thanking God for delivering me. I stand in the mirror, listening to music, seeing my glow return, sleeping peacefully again.

God never intended for me to stay broken.

That season forced me to slow down and heal what I tried to bury. I didn't just mourn the relationship—I mourned the dreams attached to it. There were nights when tears became my prayers and faith was all I had. In that brokenness, God met me with grace.

My story did not end with divorce—God only paused it to restore me.

I learned how to forgive without reconciliation.

If you are healing after divorce, know this: God still has a plan for you. You are not behind. You are not damaged. You are not disqualified from love, joy, or purpose. What broke you did not break God's promise over your life.

During my healing, God led me to create *Divorced Women's Healing Lounge*—a safe space for women to become whole again. When God brings us through something, it becomes our responsibility to help someone else.

Divorce is painful. I would never wish that kind of hurt on anyone. Writing this book was deeply therapeutic for me. Journaling had always been part of my life—perhaps God planted that seed long ago.

I never planned on writing a book. But God did.

After receiving confirmation through prayer, fasting, and a trusted friend, I began writing. Late nights, tears, reflection—and now, completion. This book had to be written.

My healing reaches completion as this book is finished and released.

My pain had a purpose—and this book is part of it.

I give all glory to God.

This chapter exists so you know you are not alone. If God brought me through betrayal, heartbreak, and pain—He can bring you through too.

To the Woman Who Is Still Crying in Her Closet

This chapter is for the woman who feels like she's losing herself while trying to hold everything together.

The woman who smiles in front of her kids but cries in the shower.

The woman who keeps forgiving someone who keeps wounding her.

The woman who loves deeply—but is tired of being hurt in silence.

Sis, I see you—because I was you.

I know what it feels like to question your worth while staying loyal to someone who is constantly showing you disloyalty. I know how confusing it is to believe in God but stay in a situation that is destroying your peace. I know how exhaustion settles into your bones when you're always "being strong" but never truly being safe.

Let me tell you something I had to learn the hard way:

God does not expect you to sacrifice your life, safety, or dignity in the name of love or faith.

Love is not chaos.

Love is not fear.

Love does not require you to endure repeated betrayal, disrespect, or emotional harm.

If someone keeps showing you who they are and you keep hoping they'll become someone else, you are carrying a burden God never gave you.

Sometimes we think staying means faith—but faith also knows when to walk away.

If you are constantly anxious, drained, checking phones, bracing yourself for lies, or shrinking to keep the peace, that is not the life God designed for you. That is survival—not love.

You don't need more patience. You don't need to forgive harder. You don't need to pray louder so they will change.

You need peace. And peace is never found in places where your soul is under constant attack.

Leaving does not make you weak. Leaving does not mean you failed. Leaving does not cancel God's grace on your life.

Sometimes God allows your heart to finally break so you stop settling for what is breaking you.

If you're in your waiting season right now, don't rush it.

Don't distract yourself from the healing.

Don't jump into another relationship hoping someone else can numb the pain.

Sit with God. Let Him undo what trauma taught you. Let Him restore your voice. Let Him rebuild your confidence. Let Him teach you discernment instead of desperation.

I promise you this:

It gets better — but only when you choose yourself.

There came a moment when I realized I could either keep surviving or finally start living. I chose to live. I chose peace. I chose God. And in doing that, I found myself again.

You will too.

If God brought me through betrayal, fear, divorce, and heartbreak, He can bring you through whatever you're facing right now.

You are not broken. You are not damaged goods. You are not behind. And you are not alone.

This chapter exists so you know that your healing matters and that walking away can be holy.

Choose peace. Choose truth. Choose yourself.

God will do the rest.

Closing Prayer

Heavenly Father,

Thank You for being my refuge in every storm and my strength when I felt weak. Thank You for carrying me through seasons of betrayal, heartbreak, and confusion, and for never leaving me when I couldn't find the words to pray. You saw every tear, heard every silent cry, and held me together when I felt shattered.

Lord, I release every ounce of pain, disappointment, and brokenness into Your hands. I forgive those who hurt me—not because they deserve it, but because You desire freedom for my heart. I let go of bitterness, fear, and shame, and I receive Your peace, healing, and restoration.

Heal every woman who is reading this book, God. Mend the broken places in her heart. Strengthen her when she feels weak. Give her clarity where there has been confusion, courage where there has been fear, and hope where there has been despair. Let her know she is not forgotten, not behind, and not disqualified from love, joy, or purpose.

Teach us to walk in discernment, to honor ourselves, to set healthy boundaries, and to trust You fully with our future. Restore what has been stolen. Renew what has been worn down. Replace pain with purpose and ashes with beauty.

Lord, thank You for turning my test into a testimony and my pain into purpose. Thank You for reminding me that my past does not define me and that my future is secure in You. I trust your timing. I trust Your plan. I trust Your heart toward me. I declare that old things have passed away, and all things are becoming new. I step forward healed, whole, and confident in who You created me to be.

In Jesus' name,

Amen.

Reference Page

Divorce women Healing Loung

The Divorced Women Healing Lounge exists to create a safe, supportive, and faith-nurtured space where divorced women can heal, rebuild, and rediscover themselves without judgment. Our mission is to empower women to release emotional burdens, break unhealthy ties, regain their confidence, and walk boldly into a renewed identity rooted in God's love.

Through community, education, encouragement, and sisterhood, we provide guidance, compassion, and practical tools that help women rise stronger, restore their worth, and step confidently into the next chapter of their lives. Membership also includes a customized gift box with gifts, and monthly give aways.

https://www.skool.com/divorced-women-healing-lounge-2601

Faith Digital products

https://admin.shopify.com/store/she-so-precious-2/products